Learning to Swim
In The
Short Sale Ocean

The ONLY Guide You Need To Navigate the Short Sale Ocean

Ben Benita

Parson's Porch & Company

Learning to Swim
In The
Short Sale Ocean

Parson's Porch Books

Learning to Swim In The Short Sale Ocean

ISBN: Softcover 978-0692390467

Copyright © 2015 by Ben Benita

To order additional copies of this book, contact:

Parson's Porch Books
1-423-475-7308
www.parsonsporch.com

Parson's Porch Books is an imprint of Parson's Porch & Company (PP&C) in Cleveland, Tennessee. PP&C is an innovative non-profit organization which raises money by publishing books of noted authors, representing all genres. All donations from contributors and profits from publishing are shared with the poor.

Foreword

This guide was written in follow-up to my best-selling book:

"Are YOU More Likely To See Bigfoot or A Short Sale Approval Letter?"

The purpose of this guide is to help Homeowners, Real Estate Agents, Attorneys, and anyone else navigate what seems like an ocean of paperwork and headaches.

What follows is taken from more than 10 years of short sale negotiations and processing, and more than 10 years of helping hundreds of Homeowners and Real Estate Agents all over the country. Much of this information comes from "off-the-record" conversations with Supervisors, Vice Presidents, and even people in the offices of the CEO and President for some of the country's largest banks.

Processing and negotiating short sales has to be the most ridiculous process on the planet. With the help of this guide, you too can make it to closing!!!

The Best Negotiation Tip I Ever Got: Negotiate Like a 4 Year Old

On a visit to an investor summit, several years ago in Maryland, I had the pleasure of meeting George Ross, Donald Trump's attorney and mentor (I also got a SWEET photo with him while I was wearing one of my stylish Hawaiian shirts).

While there he told me:

".....of all the deals I ever did with Donald, the best negotiator I have ever come across is still my 4 year old niece.....she just keeps asking and asking and asking and asking until she hears YES".

Having 3 children of my own, I can tell you, no truer words could be spoken when negotiating!!!

When dealing with banks, this is Rule #1:
- Just Keep Asking and Asking and Asking UNTIL YOU GET A "YES"!!!!

I would also like to extend a special thank you to Tracie Thomas Norman, whose contributions and efforts have helped make this book possible.

Testimonials

"Ben Benita is extremely knowledgeable on Short Sales. We have sat on Short Sale panels together and I always learn from him. His book is a wealth of information and I highly recommend it to anyone involved in Short Sales.
Bryant Tutas, Co-Founder, <u>www.ShortSaleSuperstars.com</u>

"There are only a handful of people in our industry who cannot only claim to be an "expert", but also back it up with incredible, hand on experience. Ben Benita is without a doubt one of them!"
Mike Linkenauger, Short Sale Specialist Network Director of Operations
www.Short-Sale-Specialists.com

"I have spoken to hundreds of Short Sale Professionals over the years and I must say, after many conversations with Ben, he is hands down one of the best people in the short sale space."
Randy Tobbe, Account Executive
www.RealtyCommander.com

"Ben has been an insightful industry leader in the Short Sale space for many years. As a member of many Short Sale forums he has gladly shared his tips and tricks for getting Short Sales closed! Even a seasoned Short Sale Real Estate Agent like myself still finds that I am learning something new from him all the time.

I recommend this book highly to anyone looking for the real scoop on Short Sales!"
Kevin Lancaster, Moderator
Short Sale Masterminds on Facebook

Ben is one of the best mitigation specialists in the industry. This book is a compelling look into the world of short sales negotiations and short sales.
Lee Honish, former Head Loss Mitigator
IndyMac Bank

Table of Contents

Important Terms to Know:

SHORT SALE – If you do not know what this means, you need to be REALLY thankful you have this guide!!!! As it relates to real estate, a "short sale" refers to the selling of a property for less than what is owed.

THE SERVICER – The "Servicer" is who the Homeowner writes his/her monthly mortgage payment/check to (or in many cases, who they SHOULD be writing the check to). The "Servicer" gets paid to collect mortgage payments, pay escrows for taxes and insurance, send out letters and statements to the Homeowner, HARASS THEM when they miss payments, etc.

THE INVESTOR - The entity that actually gave the cash to the homeowner to buy the house. There are 3 types of Investors:

1) - Government Backed - Fannie Mae, Freddie Mac, FHA or VA
2) – A Portfolio Loan – Where the Servicer and Investor are the same
3) – Private Investor – Deutsche Bank, I Love Short Sales Hedge Fund, etc.

Understanding the Flow of Money

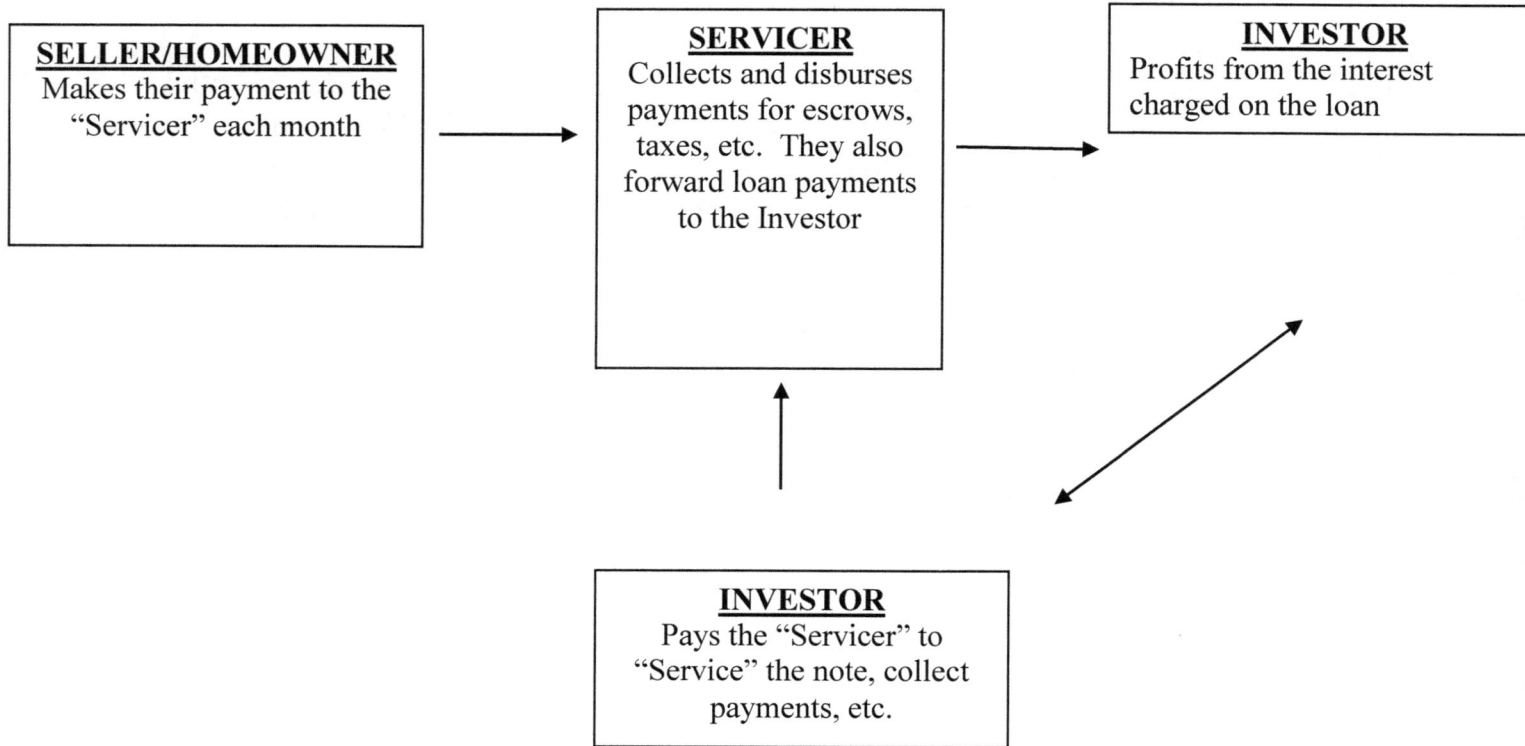

SELLER/HOMEOWNER
Makes their payment to the
"Servicer" each month

SERVICER
Collects and disburses
payments for escrows,
taxes, etc. They also
forward loan payments
to the Investor

INVESTOR
Profits from the interest
charged on the loan

INVESTOR
Pays the "Servicer" to
"Service" the note, collect
payments, etc.

Hiring Help – Do You REALLY Want To Process Short Sales?

Did you really get into real estate to sit on hold, send 100 page faxes, and argue over some of the most ridiculous policies on the planet?

In some states Agents can actually lose their license for processing and negotiating short sales, so my question –
WHY WOULD YOU DO IT?

You can spend 30-40 hours processing and negotiating a short sale (that is the average length of time it takes), OR, you can spend those 30-40 hours
Helping other homeowners
Generating MORE business
MAKING MORE MONEY

….seems a pretty easy decision!!!

What is YOUR time worth?

There is a reason when you go see a doctor that the doctor does NOT answer the phone when you call, does not check you in, does not make appointments, does not help you fill out forms, and does not send you the bill afterwards. If they did, they would not make any money. The same is true for Agents, why deal with this if you don't have to?

Is this how you want your real estate career?

When you die (yes it's gonna' happen),
Do you want your tomb stone to say?

"He Could Have REALLY Been Something"

"Please Tell Me The Number One Reason Short Sales Take Sooooo Long?"

Let's Guess:

    A) Because banks are overwhelmed – (THEY WANT YOU TO BELIEVE THIS)
    B) Because you didn't send the right documents – (THEY WILL TELL YOU THIS, BUT ALSO NOT TRUE)
    C) Because they make more money dragging out the process? – **WINNER WINNER WINNER**!!!!

Let me explain. Using the previous diagram, here is what happens:

The Investor Typically Pays Annual "Servicing Fees" To The Servicer As Follows:

- When the Seller is current and has not missed any payments, Servicers earn:
.0025% of the Loan Balance
(These are often referred to as "Performing Notes" in Banking-speak)

And

-When the Seller is NOT current and HAS missed payments, Servicers earn:

.005% Of the Loan Balance Annually (yes, typically the fees DOUBLE)!!
These are often referred to as "Non-Performing Notes" in Banking-Speak

SO……if YOU were a Servicer (Bank Of America, Wells Fargo, etc.), and you were earning DOUBLE what you typically do in revenues, exactly how hard, how efficient, how "easy", and how quick would you make the short sale process?

Have You Ever Wondered Why The Servicer Cannot Tell The Homeowner To Miss Payments?

BECAUSE THEY MAKE MORE MONEY WHEN PAYMENTS ARE MISSED!!!
It is a conflict of interest for the Investor, and as such, they can NOT tell the

Homeowner to miss payments! (As with everything in short sales, there are of course exceptions)

INTERESTING FACT – The Servicer, as part of their Loan Servicing Agreement with the Investor, gets paid even if the Seller is NOT making payments!

THINK ABOUT IT:
As soon as a short sale closes, the "Servicer" no longer earns that ¼% - ½% for "Servicing" the loan….As soon as your short sale is approved, the Servicer loses your Seller as a client, i.e., they no longer get paid for "Servicing" the note.

In the Servicer's defense (and this is the ONLY time I will defend them), who could blame them for playing games, pretending to lose documents, doing NOTHING with your short sale package and THEN telling you documents are expired? Be honest, if YOU could get away with it, exactly how hard would <u>YOU</u> work to GET RID OF A REVENUE STREAM KNOWING YOU HAVE SHAREHOLDERS TO REPORT TO?

As such, Servicers like Bank Of America, Wells Fargo, CITI, etc., have ZERO ZIPPY ZILCH NADA (for my Spanish friends) financial motivation to get your short sale approved quickly!

This is the number one reason why they drag their feet and MAKE RIDUCLOUS REQUESTS!!! It is also why you should negotiate like a 4 year old, be a TOTAL PAIN IN THEIR BACKSIDE AND FORCE THEM TO MAKE DECISIONS!!!!
GREAT TIP - The above is also why you should ALWAYS try to find out who the Investor is on the loan. The Investor DOES care how long this process takes….. Contact them to tell them their Servicer is playing games and charging them "Unnecessary Servicing Fees"

AND YOUR SHORT SALE WILL GET DONE!!!

One of the BEST email subject lines you can use (see more at the end of this guide):

"Why Are You Letting -Servicer- (Bank of America, Wells Fargo, etc?????) Charge You Unnecessary Servicing Fees?"

If you put that email subject line in a message TO the Investor, and "cc" EVERYONE at the Servicing bank, you WILL get a response!!!!

Want To Know The #2 Reason Short Sales Get Delayed?

Here is a BIGGER SHOCKER THAN OLD FASHIONED CASHOLA:

PEOPLE ARE LAZY!!!!!

The Negotiators, their supervisors, Team leads and VP's are all human and most are simply lazy!!!

When short sales ARE approved, there is a LARGE list of disclosures and documents that the Servicer MUST send to the Investor explaining what happened with the short sale and why.

If, however, the short sale is denied, gets "kicked-out", or goes to foreclosure, NO MORE PAPERWORK!!! Your file goes from loss mitigation to the foreclosure or REO Department.

Think about it. If you get frustrated, you give up and go away.
Most agents will simply tell the Seller the bank will not cooperate, sorry.

FACT - It is simply easier to irritate you and let the home go to foreclosure than it is for them to approve the short sale.

What happens to your short sale file when it IS closed, when it IS denied, or, when it DOES go to foreclosure?

BYE BYE

It gets DELETED from loss mitigation and now becomes an issue for the foreclosure and/or REO (Real Estate Owned) department!!!

REMEMBER – People at the bank GET PAID NO MATTER WHAT HAPPENS WITH YOUR SHORT SALE!!!!

Understanding Investor Losses

Generally speaking, it is typically in the Investor's best interest to complete a short sale for two reasons:

1) Foreclosure Holding Costs - The Investor will typically lose 20 - 40% MORE when they are stuck with a foreclosure (they must pay attorneys to foreclose, then cover taxes, insurance, utilities, HOA fees, general maintenance, etc.). Also general liability. If your Seller owns the property, the general liability falls on them.

There are of course exceptions. Occasionally an Investor actually makes MORE money foreclosing, but this is generally not the case unless mortgage insurance is in place. When there is, in SOME cases, the Investor on the note actually makes MUCH more money via foreclosure (this is why you should ALWAYS ask if Mortgage Insurance exists). We will touch on this later, but just like any "insurance", the Investor gets a check to cover a portion of their losses.

2) Loan Loss Reserves – This is somewhat advanced, but you made it this far, so YOU must be somewhat advanced (and I know most people will never actually read this). Banks are required to set aside funds any time a loan goes delinquent (remember, banks make money investing and placing funds). When payments are delinquent, a bank's "Loan Loss Reserve" kicks in and banks are REQUIRED to set aside anywhere from one to eight times the loan amount to cover any potential losses.

In "Laymen's Term" – if your seller has a $200,000 loan, and he/she goes delinquent, a bank with a 2X Loan Loss Reserve now MUST set aside $400,000 (2 X $200,000) to cover the potential future loss. This means there is $400,000 that can NOT be loaned out for car loans, credit cards, other mortgages etc., until the bad debt is cleared off the books. Every day that $400,000 is tied up, is a day that the bank COULD be otherwise making money lending those funds.

This is also why you will ALWAYS see an "uptick" in short sale approvals in December as banks attempt to "clear the books" and get that money out working for them again.

Short Sale Versus Foreclosure, From the Seller's Perspective

Generally speaking, it is often best for the Seller to do a short sale, here's why:

A Short Sale itself is much less detrimental to the Seller's credit. It allows you the opportunity to settle any outstanding balances. A short sale also avoids the embarrassment of having a foreclosure or "For Sale" sign in the yard.

As with anything in life, there are cases where a Seller's credit is already ruined (or they just don't care), and where heavy financial distress exists. For these Sellers it may actually make financial sense for the Seller to live in the home without sending in payments for as long as possible. Let the lender foreclose then get paid to move out (often referred to as "cash for keys").

I have personally on at least four cases where the Seller had not made a payment in MORE THAN 5 YEARS!!!!

Bankruptcy may also be a wise option as this can allow a Seller to further extend their "free-time" in the property.

As you work on more and more short sales, you will find that each short sale, each Seller, each situation varies greatly.

Though we all want to get paid, in the end, it is always best to do what is in the best interest of the Seller.

Great Tip – Bankruptcy attorneys are a GREAT source of referrals!!!

Missing Payments
My Thoughts

JOKE TIME - Ever want to know if anyone cares, try missing a mortgage payment!!!!

I have been doing short sales for many many years and so far, the MOST payments I have seen missed to date – 68!!!!!

You will hear a TON of varying opinions on this topic. My two-cents, after having done short sale processing and negotiations for more than nine years are as follows:

I have been told agents cannot legally tell homeowners to stop paying their mortgage (even in cases where it is CLEARLY in the Homeowner's best financial interest….particularly where they are BORROWING money to keep up, only going further and further into debt)

However, you can tell Homeowners the ONLY financial benefit they get by sending in payments is that it will maintain their credit and prevent 30, 60, 90 day lates from showing up on credit reports. There are certain Investor guidelines, FHA for example, that state a Seller must be behind on payments at time of closing.

I often simply have this conversation with Homeowners:

Me: "So Mr. Homeowner, how much are your monthly mortgage payments?"
Homeowner – "$1500/month"

Me: "If I told you about a web site called www.KeepMyCredit.com, and you could go there and pay $1500 month, to keep your credit where it is RIGHT NOW, would you go there and pay $1500/month"
Homeowners (at least most) – "NOPE"!!!

Though a sarcastic truth – Financially, for most homeowners they might as well send their check directly to Experian, Equifax, or Trans Union, the three national credit reporting agencies, as they would get the exact same benefit!!!!

The homeowner might actually do even better sending the money directly to a charity they support, here's why:

<u>Not Only Would They Still Get The Tax Deduction, But The Charity Will Actually Thank Them For The Money!!!!</u>

<u>Ask The Homeowners: "When Was The Last Time Your Servicer Thanked You For Sending In A Payment?!?"</u>

Keep sending cashola to a loan Servicer on an over-financed property, and not only will you NEVER receive a "thank you", but your Homeowner WILL NEVER SEE a DIME OF THAT MONEY AGAIN!!!!

When Sellers are fearful of their credit and want to keep making payments ask them: "What is more important to you today? Your credit score or the financial wellbeing of you and your family".

Or this one:

"Would you sleep better at night knowing you have $5000 cash in the bank from skipped mortgage payments or knowing you have a good credit score but no cash....?"

Or

"Do you have cash saved up for when it is time to move, pay movers, pay security deposits, first month's rent, etc.?"

Missing payments is NOT necessarily for everyone, but if your client is behind on payments already, using a credit card, savings, or otherwise borrowing money, find a careful way to get them to stop (at a minimum suggest they start saving some money to move)!!!

Quick Story:

A story in the Washington Post newspaper a few years ago featured a couple in Montgomery County Maryland who had purchased a brand new home for roughly $700,000. After a short time, the builder, with the market beginning to crash, was offering the EXACT same home with a finished basement on a nicer lot for just under $500,000....

That is $200,000 LESS THAN WHAT THEY OWED for those keeping track at home.

Do you know what this couple did?   They put a contract on one of the new homes, (again, the EXACT same model with a finished basement and better lot), closed on the property, then mailed their keys back to their lender (this is known as "jingle mail") with a note that said:

"For $200,000, you can have this house!"

Is that the "right thing" to do? It depends who you ask?

Ask your lender and they will tell you -- *"NEVER DO THAT"*

Ask me - I will tell you without hesitation:

"FINANCIALLY IT IS THE RIGHT THING TO DO EVERY TIME!!!!

In 10 to 15 years they will likely be able to pull several hundred thousand dollars in equity from their new home rather than just be "back to even"……..hard to argue against that!!!

Should You Even Bother With The Short Sale Listing? How to Pre-Screen Clients

Ok, so you now know why you have been getting push back from the bank? Now you must decide whether or not to take that short sale listing? We all want to help Sellers and get paid; HOWEVER, no one wants to spend 3-6 months on a short sale and have it be a complete waste of time!!!

There are few things worse than having several months of work into a short sale and not having it close because of the Seller.

I have included a *"Pre-Listing Questionnaire"* in the "Sample Documents" Section of this book

Be sure to use this always and with every listing!!!!

GREAT TIP FOR WINNING A LISTING:

A "Do Not Call Letter" – Have your Seller fill this out if he/she is getting OBNOXIOUS collection calls, no other agents are offering this
(See "Sample Documents" Below)

A couple in Florida recently sued Bank of America and received $1,000,000 for continuing to contact a Seller AFTER they had been instructed not to.

Loan Modification – Would Your Client Prefer To Keep Their Home?

Questions To Ask:

1) Are you currently working or will you be in the near future?
2) Do you have an adjustable rate mortgage that is about to adjust?
3) Are you currently behind one or more house payments?
4) Is your mortgage a "Pick-A-Pay" or "Negative Amortization" loan?
5) Do you owe more than your home is worth?

There are really only a few factors that go into decisioning a loan modification.

Generally speaking, you need to think of them as a refinance.

The Homeowner:

SHOULD have current continued income, And…

SHOULD be able to show hardship, And…

SHOULD show monthly expenses are generally 10% - 30% higher than their income.

If your client meets these general criteria, he/she may be able to keep their home through modification.

There are a number of different government and investor specific programs, but, your client needs to be realistic about his or her situation.

Joke Time

My Seller did a debt consolidation…..now they only have one bill they are not paying!!!!!

Setting Expectations: Realistic Time Frames

Short sales should rarely take more than 60-90 days to complete once all documents are in to the bank. ASSUMING you have a complete package, a good offer, and a ready, willing, (and patient) Buyer!!!

Once all documents are collected, you can expect:

ACTION	TIME FRAME
Short sale packet is faxed to lender and confirmed RECEIVED	1 to 10 Days
Short sale packet is processed, negotiator is assigned	1 to 30 Days
Broker's Price Opinion (BPO) or Appraisal is ordered	1 to 21 Days
BPO or Appraisal is returned to the Negotiator	2 to 10 Days
Negotiator confirms offer meets short sale acceptance guidelines and is submitted to Investor for approval	1 to 21 Days
Acceptance Letter issued	1 to 30 Days
TOTAL AVERAGE TIME FOR ACCEPTANCE	45 to 90 Days

Going over the above will save both you and your client LOTS of headaches and, set a reasonable foundation for expectations. As you will learn, many banks are now REQUIRED to give you an answer within 60 days of receiving a complete short sale package!!

Three Most Important Things to Know Before Sending in the Short Sale Packet:

1) **<u>Who Is The Investor?</u>** - We put this first because there is NO other piece of information that is more important to the success of your short sale. The Investor guidelines will not only dictate what "NET" or "Payoff" you need to get to the Investor, but it will also tell you what documents are needed, if the Seller can get relocation assistance, and HOW MUCH COMMISSION YOU CAN GET AS THE AGENT (some banks pay 8% - 10% commission, keep reading, we will tell)!!

To find out who the investor is, try asking your Negotiator:

> Is this a Portfolio Loan – meaning it is held by the Servicer?
> Is this a Government Backed loan – Fannie Mae, Freddie Mac, etc?
> Is the investor on this Private, is it held by a Private Investor (these can be tricky)

Some negotiators will tell you they cannot disclose the above; HOWEVER, it is not true, they absolutely CAN answer these 3 questions.

If the loan is "Portfolio", then the Servicer, who the Seller writes his/her check to, owns and likely funded the note.

If the loan is "Government Backed, or GSE Loan", it is most likely Fannie Mae or Freddie Mac. You can visit these web sites to verify:

> Freddie Mac - https://ww3.freddiemac.com/loanlookup/

Or

> Fannie Mae - https://www.knowyouroptions.com/loanlookup

If you discover your Seller's loan is a VA Loan, this is referred to as a "VA Compromise Sale" where the VA will actually pay the difference between what is owed and what the home sells for. These generally go very quickly and can be a blessing to get done.

If the loan is held by a Private Investor, you may have a few challenges, below are the steps to overcome them:

a) This information SHOULD be in the loan documents your Seller filled out, this can be a HUGE pain in the _____ to dig through, but, it is in there

b) Have your Seller send in a Qualified Written Request, "QWR" (see "Sample Documents"), asking the Servicer who the Private Investor is on the note.

c) You can try MERS (Mortgage Electronic Registration Systems):

> https://www.mers-servicerid.org/sis/.
> Or call them directly – 800-646-MERS (6377)

One of the many great reasons to k now who the Investor is, it will help you determine the Minimum Net Requirement, or "MNR", the amount needed for an approval. Here is the generally accepted percentage of Broker's Price Opinion Value for approvals (so you know where your "net" to the bank needs to be):

> Fannie Mae (FNMA) – 92% of BPO
> Freddie Mac – 92% of BPO
> VA Loan – 88% of BPO
> FHA – 88%, 86%, 84% of BPO depending on time frames
> Conventional – 75% – 95% of BPO
> Second Liens – 5% - 10% of the amount owed
> Third and other Liens – 5% - 10% of the amount owed

2) **Is the current loan FHA?** – If so, ask the Servicer for a copy of HUD Form 90045, this shows Seller eligibility and pricing recommendation and the MNR needed for approval. This Form is also referred to as the Approval to Participate, or "ATP".

3) **Is there Mortgage Insurance (MI) on the loan** – if there is, you could be facing an uphill battle. Find out who the MI company is and make note, you may need it later. Also find out what the Coverage Ratio is for the loss, as this too will help you calculate where your NET offer needs to be.

The Most Powerful Document in Short Sales – The Qualified Written Request

Per RESPA - "ANY request, written and signed by the Seller is deemed to be a Qualified Written Request, or "QWR"."

If a Seller requests anything in writing, Investor information, Mortgage Insurer information, copies of documents, etc., the Servicer MUST acknowledge and respond to this request, or be in direct violation of RESPA Section 6 (12USC 2605).

<u>When these are requests MOST useful:</u>
1 – Finding out who the Investor is – VERY VERY VERY helpful when negotiating and when issues arise…..and issues WILL arise!!!
And
2 – Finding out who the Mortgage Insurance Company is - Again, this can affect Minimum Net Requirements as well as approval time frames.

Some things in life are simply a MUST, things you just should do, like:

1) Wearing pants to work (there are exceptions, but in general…)

2) Wearing pants when there is snow on the ground (again, there are exceptions when this is funny, but in general)

3) FINDING OUT WHO THE INVESTOR IS ON A SHORT SALE. If you want to solve 90% of your short sale problems, and CLOSE 90% or more of your short sales, knowing who the DECISION MAKER, who the Investor is, this is just an absolute MUST!!!

Designing the Perfect
Short Sale Packet

So you have elected to move forward with your short sale. You know who the Investor/Decision maker is. You have learned the client is on board and it is in their best interest to complete a short sale. The heat is on and now they are counting on you to make it happen!!!

THINGS TO DO BEFORE SENDING IN THE SHORT SALE PACKET:

1) Call the Servicer and ask these 2 questions:
"What is the correct fax number to send in my short sale packet" (you may want to call twice)
And,
"What SPECIFICALLY is needed in the packet" (many servicers now require specific bank documents and addendums to be signed and sent in)

2) Be certain to put the account number ON TOP OF ALL PAGES BEING SENT – most documents get imaged and you will get imaged MUCH more quickly if you have account numbers on top of each page.

3) Send in your OWN BPO Letter (see "Sample Documents" below) – Tell the bank what you think about the market, inventory in your area, property condition, comparable sales, etc.

4) If your client is receiving harassing phone calls, send in a Do Not Call Letter (see "Sample Documents"). Tell the lender additional calls are in direct violation of Fair Debt Collection Practices Act 805(c) (your Seller will LOVE you for this)

5) On your Preliminary Settlement Statement:

a) ALWAYS over estimate taxes, insurance, HOA Fees, etc. Your short sale will ALWAYS take longer than you think….allow for this.

b) When first and second liens are involved, the best strategy is to send in two different Preliminary Settlement Statements:

For the First Lien Settlement Statement – Offer the second lien only 25% of what is owed. If questioned, tell the first lien you are fairly confident the second lien will accept this amount.

For the Second Lien Settlement Statement – Offer the second lien only $3000. Again if questioned, tell the second lien you are fairly confident the first lien will pay them this amount.

c) Include a payment to you for negotiating the short sale (assuming you are cray enough to do this on your own, why should you work extra and NOT get paid for it). Be sure to clear this with your Broker and as always, disclose this to the Seller.

d) Ask for "Seller Relocation Assistance" – FHA, the HAFA Program ($10,000 currently) and most banks allow this (your Seller will be VERY glad you did)!!!
e) Partner with a local real estate attorney –Are YOU really qualified to give legal advice on financial matters? They are also great referral sources!

6) On ANY AND EVERY cover sheet and e-mail you send in, tell the Servicer where they can send your short sale approval letter, and thank them for all of their time and hard work. There are few things worse than having an acceptance letter ready and the Servicer not knowing where to send it.

AGAIN - ALWAYS ALWAYS ALWAYS ASK THE BANK FOR "RELOCATION ASSISTANCE"!!! Most banks will pay at least $3000 to the Seller (or tenant) to move, and some banks pay more than $30,000!!!!!

Getting the Packet to the Servicer

Well it sure SEEMS simple; HOWEVER, packets and documents get lost all the time. We suggest you call the Servicer TWICE to get the best fax number to send in your packet and also send it by email where possible. Call no more than 48 hours after sending in your packet to confirm receipt.

OF NOTE - DO NOT BE SURPRISED IF EACH TIME YOU CALL IN YOU ARE GIVEN A DIFFERENT FAX NUMBER TO SEND THE PACKET TO. Simply fax the packet to BOTH/ALL numbers and begin follow up calls within 48 hours.

Using Equator – For short sale tracking and communication, many Servicers are now using a web site known as:

www.Equator.com

Certain short sales will be REQUIRED to go through Equator. We have found this to be beneficial at times, and a NIGHTMARE on other occasions. Be sure to ask your Servicer if your file must go through this site.

Even if your file IS running through Equator, be sure to call in at least once per week to ask about foreclosure sale dates and Service Release dates.

Dealing With "Jacque S", The Bank's Negotiator

If you have NOT yet met Jacque S., you will.....no matter the Servicer, at some point YOU TOO WILL MEET HIM!!!

He seems to work at every bank and is VERY good at his job. When handling Jacque S. you must know what to say and what not to say.

If you upset him he can ruin your deal, make him happy and he can get you paid!!!

Please print out the sentence below and place it over your computer (or stamp it on your forehead):

The People I Call In Loss Mitigation Are Called "Negotiators" For A Reason: They Get Paid To Negotiate With Me!

They Get Paid To Tell Me "No" (It Is Right There In The Phone Script They Read From When I Call Them)

Negotiators get paid to tell you "NO", not enough cashola, try again (it is right there in the phone script they read to you from, sentence number one in their job description)!!!!

Interesting Fact:

Some negotiators ACTUALLY GET IN TROUBLE IF THEY ACCEPT YOUR FIRST OFFER!!!

Who Are These "Negotiators"? - Most are paid hourly. They sit in a cubicle playing video games, watching porn, (yeah, porn, I said it), they are on Facebook, texting boyfriends or girlfriends, etc. all day long.

When you call in, most do not want to help or talk to you......who can really blame them?

Remember, as with ANY negotiation, it is of utmost importance to get your negotiator ON YOUR SIDE.......MAKE CERTAIN getting you an acceptance letter is as easy as possible by showing them what a great offer you have.

Great ice breakers for making your negotiator your friend:

"Where are you located?"
"Don't you hate these things?"
"At least we have a job?"
"How long have you been working there?"
"How many files do you have?"
"How many have you closed?"

With sarcasm – "Don't you enjoy asking, or being asked, the same questions everyday?"

Ever wonder why banks can record calls and you cannot (b/c they have no fiduciary responsibility to you, i.e., they can lie but call it "negotiating"!!!

Most of what the negotiators tell you (and often state as "fact") is just pre-scripted bull---- or pre-scripted horse---- (choose your farm animal).

The average length of employment for a short sale negotiator is only two to four months.   9 out of 10 calls they get are from attorneys, agents, and other persons complaining to them about the short sale process…a process the Negotiator has virtually no control over.

Want to know what happens when they get tired of hearing you and everyone else complain and they just quit?
Your file then goes to someone else who is over-worked and:

You may have to START YOUR SHORT SALE COMPLETELY OVER, Or, You hear "Documents Are Missing" even though 2 days earlier they had EVERYTHING!!!

Calling – Call not less than once per week (this will come in VERY when it comes time to escalate, and, will also make your Seller happy knowing you are being pro-active for his or her benefit.) Be sure your Seller is aware of EVERY correspondence you make with the Servicer.

As soon as possible, be sure to "escalate" your file, or have the Negotiator open an escalation (that means, MAKE YOUR FILE A PRIORITY). This can this can be after 30 days, 45, days, 60 days, it varies by lender (See "Escalation Section" below) When we say "escalate", we mean go directly to Supervisors, Vice Presidents, contact the Office of the CEO and President, and reach out directly to the Investor on the loan.

Always, With Any Negotiation, Make It Easy For The Other Side To Say "Yes"!!!

Hot Tip:

In short sales you want to speak with the people that WRITE the scripts, the ones that make the rules……. NOT the people that READ FROM the scripts and are TOLD WHAT THE RULES ARE!!

Are you speaking to the executive level people, the decision makers, and the people that WRITE the scripts?

Much like buying a car, you can deal with the salesperson who must ask "permission" to approve your offer, or you can ask to speak to the manager, the REAL decision maker, in order to get things done!!!

Remember This:

EVERYTHING on a short sale is negotiable, commissions, closing costs……EVERYTHING!!!

Story:

We got a short sale approved where the Seller literally had just over $8000 to his name (he had lost his job and was living off of this savings).

When we received the approval letter, the bank REQUIRED him to bring $14,000 CASH TO CLOSING!!!!

After MANY phone calls I got the Vice President of the bank on the phone and said "Please Explain"!!!

Here is what he told me:

"Ben, if we ask 100 people, with $8000 in the bank, to bring $14,000 cash to closing, and ONLY 10 people do, that is $140,000 we will get…..money we would never see IF WE DIDN'T ASK!!!"

Think about it…..if you don't ask, you don't get!!!

Negotiator Contact Information

GETTING YOUR NEGOTIATOR'S DIRECT PHONE NUMBER AND E-MAIL ADDRESS IS A MUST (of course if you are working with us we likely already have contact information)

Here are some tips for getting it:

1) Just ask your negotiator for it:

"I am hard to reach by phone, e-mail is best. Can I have your e-mail address Mr. Negotiator?"

2) If they say no, get the correct spelling of their first and last name. Most e-mails strings are:

Firstname.lastname@Servicername.com

If this does not work, the other e-mail string is often:

Firstname.middleinitial.lastname@Servicername.com

BEST TRICK:

If you have your negotiator's first and last name, simply send an e-mail to yourself, with a "cc" to:

Firstname.a.lastname@bankname.com
Firstname.b.lastname@bankname.com
Firstname.c.lastname@bankname.com

All the way through the alphabet. You will get 25 e-mails with "bad e-mail address", but, you will also get 1 that goes through.....make note of it!!!

Once you confirm a negotiator is assigned to your file, you will also NEED to know the contact information for his/her supervisor, to get this:

Call Loss Mitigation and ask for Supervisor Contact Information:

OBJECTION – I cannot give you the Supervisor's name

OVERCOMING THE OBJECTION - Call Customer Service, Accounting, Human Resources (these numbers are readily available online), and say:

"I am sorry, I was trying to reach a supervisor for loss mitigation or for _____ (your rep). I must have been transferred to you on accident. Can you tell me the name/number/e-mail (whatever you are seeking) for _____"

If THEY Object or ask why you need a supervisor:

"I was told _____ (my rep.) is out of town, busy, etc. and this home is facing foreclosure. It is VERY urgent that I speak with someone that can help our mutual client."

It works. Most of these departments do not get calls like this and most are VERY VERY helpful..........Git R' Done!!!!

It has been our experience that the above works almost every time. As always, if the person who answers the phone is not cooperative, CALL BACK!!!! Most of these lenders are HUGE and you never get the same person twice. When you call, be VERY, VERY, VERY polite and most will help.

Remember - People in Human Resources, Accounting etc. are seldom given phone scripts to read from......i.e., THEY ARE **NOT** TOLD TO **NOT** GIVE OUT SUPERVISOR AND EXECUTIVE CONTACT INFORMATION.

Negotiations - Whoever Has the Leverage - Wins

We have all heard – "Whoever has the money makes the rules."

Translation – "Whoever Has The 'LEVERAGE' Makes The Rules!"

In any short sale, whoever controls the property controls the transaction.

NEVER EVER EVER EVER EVER EVER EVER EVER FORGET THIS!!
(PRINT THIS AND PUT IT OVER YOUR DESK)

As long as you and the homeowner control whether or not the home goes to foreclosure – YOU HAVE THE LEVERAGE!!!

The Investor will typically lose 20% - 40% MORE by going to foreclosure!!!
(They have to pay attorneys to foreclose, then after taking back the property, THEY must pay water, gas, electric, HOA, taxes, insurance, etc.)

Leverage from the bank's side – TIME

In ANY negotiation - the more time you have in to the transaction, the more likely you are to give in. When banks play games, lose documents, and drag out the process, you have more and more time invested. What happens?

The bank wants to cut your commission –
YOU usually do b/c you are tired of dealing with it
Or
The bank wants more money –
YOU usually give it to them b/c you are tired of dealing with it

Banks KNOW this!!! Just as you are reading the guide, banks have teams of attorneys working 100+ hour weeks to get as much money as possible from you!

The Broker's Price Opinion (BPO)

NOTHING, and I mean NOTHING is more important to your short sale's success than having an accurate BPO or appraisal completed (be certain to send in your own with your short sale packet). An unrealistic valuation will kill a short sale quicker than anything (in California there are actually laws where BPO agents can lose their license with inaccurate valuations)

KEEP IN MIND, MANY BPO AGENTS BELIEVE THEY WILL GET THE LISTING IF THE PROPERTY GOES TO FORECLOSURE (and some actually do). As such, they often have little motivation to help you. A great way to find out if this MIGHT be an issue, try asking the BPO agent:

"Are you a listing agent as well?"

Or

"Have you ever listed REO PROPERTIES?"

For most BPO's, the BPO Agent only gets $50 - $150 per valuation, never leaves his/her car (some never leave their office), and merely do a drive-by, or pull the listing and comparable sales. Who can really blame them, they are barely getting gas money to do these!!!

In order to get a realistic valuation, you should ALWAYS meet the BPO Agent at the property (a good trick, once the property goes under contract, REMOVE the lockbox so the BPO Agent MUST contact you for access).

When meeting BPO agent, be certain to bring:

1 – Copy of Hardship Letter (put this on top and READ IT to the BPO agent)
2 -- Copy of the current Sales Contract
3 -- Copy of the current Listing for the property showing price and DOM (Days on Market)
4 -- Comparable, point out any current REO property this might compete with
5 -- BPO Letter you sent in with your packet, showing what YOU think the home should be listed for in order to sell in 30 days
6 - Repair list, where applicable (and note which repairs are "insurable")

ALWAYS ALWAYS - <u>Make certain YOU are the point of contact for BPO access and insist on an interior BPO.</u>

This will insure you are able to give the BPO agent YOUR packet, and, you will now have a record and point of reference if you ever hear the Servicer tell you:

"Hi _____ (you), we never received the BPO valuation….."

If you are the point of contact, and met the agent as we recommend, you can respond with:

"Really, I met the BPO Agent at the property on _____ (date), what do you think happened to his/her valuation?

GOOD TO KNOW - Landsafe is the name of a company that does BPO's for most Servicers, including Bank of America.
For more BPO agent information, check out www.NABPOP.com

Your offer to the Servicer will be evaluated against:
1) The Offer To Value, or "OTV" - The Investor's appraisal or BPO valuation compared to your gross offer
2) The Net To Value, or "NTV" – Your NET offer compared to the BPO value
3) The Overall Loss – The Investor's acceptable percentage of total loss, or, the total amount owed compared to the NET you are offering (this varies by county and reflects the "average loss" in that county)

Understand there are 3 levels of acceptance:

Tier I Approval – meets one of the criteria above
Tier II Approval – meets two of the criteria above
Tier III Approval – meets three of the criteria above

Commission Secret Is Revealed

Chase and CITI – For their Portfolio Loans, will pay up to 8% commission as long as they meet their MNR "Minimum Net Requirement" and "8% Commission" is noted in the Listing Agreement

Wells Fargo – For their Portfolio Loans, will pay up to 10% commission, but they too need to hit their MNR and also see it noted on the Listing Agreement

Another IMPORTANT COOMMISSION NOTE – For lower priced properties, those that sell for less than $50,000, most banks WILL pay a $2500 MINIMUM commission, YOU JUST GOTTA' ASK!!!

We sold one with a $22,000 sales price and got the agents $2500 in commission......that is 11.3%!!!!!!

<u>You're Welcome:</u>
<u>Price Of Admission COVERED!!!!</u>

So You Finally Have Your Short Sale Approved, You Are Ready To Close…..Almost

So you FINALLY got your Short Sale Approval Letter and you are ready to close, don't forget:

ON YOUR APPROVAL LETTER YOU MUST CONFIRM:

1) Do the numbers on your acceptance letter match your offer and sales contract?

2) Does the Homeowner approve of the short sale consequences? Even though we KNOW they will because you pre-screened them and told them about these consequences, it is still a good idea to have your client, preferably with his/her attorney, review the approval letter

Where Will Your Seller Live After Closing?

Don't forget, your Seller will need to find a new place to live, do NOT wait until last minute to do this!!!! You don't want to work on a short sale for 5 months THEN find out your Seller has no place to live after closing…..ask me how we first learned this!!!!

Title Companies, Where to Close

You only want to work with a title company familiar with the short sale process. Make this a habit, and INSIST all of your Seller's close here. You will save yourself HOURS of time and hassle "educating" every title company you work with.

Most states allow the Buyer to choose a title company, HOWEVER, the Seller can also choose where he/she closes. When they close at separate title companies, this is known as a "split settlement" and can be a NIGHTMARE.

When your Buyer's agent wants to close elsewhere, respond with:

"Mr. /Mrs. Agent, I have been working with _____ (Title Company) during this process and feel it only fair to continue to use their services. They have ordered and reviewed title and working with them will help lead to a smoother closing. Assuming fees are the same, we both know Buyers NEVER care where they close and are always steered and directed by their agent. Let's just close with my title company since they are reasonably priced and already familiar with this short sale. That makes the most sense doesn't it?" (Always end with a question leading to "yes")

Be sure to put in the MLS:
"Seller prefers to close with _____ (title company), as they have assisted with preliminary title work and lien clearing"

The reason for this again? You do NOT want to spend hours and hours of YOUR VALUABLE TIME educating the Buyer's title company about short sales….battling the banks is headache enough!!!!

When You Have Problems,
And You Will Have Problems

One of our best advertisements:

"If you are having trouble with your short sales, call me, if you are not, call me and tell me how you do it!!!"

Notice we call this WHEN you have problems, and not IF you have problems.

When you get to the point where your negotiator is ignoring you, your fax was lost AGAIN, it's time to turn up the heat. Calling them 3 times per day at this point is IDEAL....leave strong but kind messages:
"I know you are busy, but,"
Or
"I can only imagine how many calls you get, but.............."

If they continue to ignore you, TIME TO ESCALATE YOUR FILE!!!

Some of the BEST ADVICE I ever got was to make it a practice to escalate your file as quickly as possible in order to get an acceptance letter. By "escalate", I mean contacting the corporate and/or executive offices and letting them have it!!!

I have been doing loan modifications and short sales for homeowners for several years and though not always, MOST of the time, one or two calls into the right people in the executive will GET THINGS DONE!!!

BEST ESCALATION MOVE – Contact the Investor directly, make THEM aware of what is going on and watch how things get done!!!

Escalation Example:

We recently had a homeowner who had tried for 4 months to complete a loan modification on her own with Aurora Loan Servicing. After having been LIED to and offered many broken promises, we actually GOT HER MODIFICATION ACCEPTED WITH ONE PHONE CALL!!! That's right, ONE PHONE CALL to the corporate offices (she even had a foreclosure auction date scheduled)!!!

When calling the "Big Dogs" (CEO, President, VP, etc.), it is best to call BEFORE 9AM or AFTER 5:30PM as most of these guys get in early and stay late (they will often have "underlings" answering the phone during business hours). You can often catch them before 9AM and after 5:30PM b/c they tend to work longer hours.

If done properly, an escalation SHOULD get you some type of response within 48 hours. Again, be "Professionally Aggressive".
Some of the BEST phone calls you will ever get from your negotiator doing short sales: "Hey_____ (you), you didn't have to call my boss and get me in trouble!!!"

GREAT TIP - Sending flowers or doughnuts to your negotiator or their office will also get you a response (balloons seem to work best because they are VERY noticeable). It may cost you $50 but, if you are looking at a $10,000 check, spending $50 for $10,000 is a great investment!!!

ALWAYS ALWAYS ALWAYS REMEMBER –
NEGOTIATE LIKE A 4-Year Old!!!!

BE A TOTAL PAIN IN THE ASS!!!!
(you can find my "political correctness" on page 347….that's right, it does not exist in the short sale world)!!!

Anyone high up the food chain will respect your persistence and your desire to help the homeowner…..their MUTUAL CLIENT!!!

From Winston Churchill – NEVER NEVER NEVER GIVE-UP!!!!!

Top 3 Reasons Short Sales Do Not Close, And What to Do About It

REASON #1 - First and second liens do not agree on payoffs.

Solution 1 – If the numbers are close:

1) As the Listing Agent, ask the Buyer to increase his/her offer or bring cash to closing, ALWAYS ask the Buyer first.
2) Have the Buyer increase the purchase price, keeping the "net" to the Investor the same.
3) Seller brings cash to closing.
4) Agent can contribute cash from commissions.

Solution 2 – If the numbers are WAY off and/or THERE IS NO CASH TO GIVE:

Note - ALWAYS take the position that you are a "middleman (or middle-woman)", which makes the negotiator think you are in the same boat as them....."Just stuck in the middle trying to get this off your desk":

1) "I spoke to my broker. She asked me to ask you how long you will keep the file open while we search for a new Buyer, someone that will cover that difference"

Or, particularly now,

2) "Wow, $50k to release the lien? We actually have a closing date set for the end of this month. My broker wanted me to ask if we are really going to have to cancel that scheduled closing"

Or

3) "$50k to release the lien, WOW.....I have closed many of these and never seen a second actually get $50k, is that the least the investor will take, I do not want to waste everyone's time on this if that is a firm offer?"

Or

4) If you have SOME cash, from Buyer, Seller, agents, etc., try -
"I can get you $XXX cash now to release the lien, if not, I will have to tell the Buyer to withdraw"

Or

5) If responding via e-mail/fax, start with - "Great News, I was able to get you $XXXX toward that $50k, will your investor at least consider this"

Or

6) When the above has failed, send an e-mail to the Seller with a "cc" to EVERYONE you can find at the Servicer:

"Dear ____ (Seller), because the second line wants an exhorbant amount of cash, $50,000, we are going to have to advise you to seek legal counsel about just letting the home going to foreclosure. The GOOD news, the bank will actually PAY YOU to move out after the foreclosure auction (this is referred to as "cash for keys").

In the meantime, **keep living in the home for free** until they do decide to foreclose. Sorry we were unable to help......." Again, this is generally after some of the above have not worked out and you have nothing to lose

Or

7) You can use my personal favorite (though I have NOT yet had the chance to use it):

"Dear _____ (Servicer),

With all due respect, on behalf of my client and I, would you PLEASE GET YOUR HEAD OUT OF YOUR _____ SO WE CAN GET THIS DONE!!!"

If you ever send that one, PLEASE "cc" me on the e-mail, I would LOVE LOVE LOVE to see it go out!!!

REASON #2 – The Agent Gave Up (DO NOT LET ME HEAR YOU GAVE UP ON YOUR CLIENT....EVER)!!!!

Possible Solutions –

1) RE-READ THIS BOOK or call us to help! There is no reason an agent should EVER give up on his/her client

REASON #3 – Unmotivated Seller (won't agree to promissory note, becomes non-responsive, files for bankruptcy, etc.)

Possible Solution
1) Pre-screen your clients using our "Pre-Listing Questionnaire" below
2) Make CERTAIN to keep your Seller engaged and updated during the process

REASON #3.5 – Buyer Walks

Possible Solution –

1) As noted above, make certain to keep your Buyer and his/her agent involved and updated.

2) We ALWAYS suggest taking back-up contracts and consider working with investors

REASON 3.6 – Foreclosure, it happens

Possible Solutions –

1) These happen...stay on top of your file and foreclosure dates, escalate EVERY short sale as soon as possible......ALWAYS ask if there is a foreclosure date when you call in for updates

Overcoming Agent Issues

As a real estate agent, or ANYONE NEGOTIATING SHORT SALES, you will have countless problems throughout the process. Here are a few of the more common and how to overcome them:

1) **PROBLEM – "The Servicer is taking FOREVER to make a decision"**

How to Solve:

Before blasting your negotiator (and you will RARELY hear me stick up for them), keep in mind your negotiator has NO control over time frames and can only communicate what you tell him/her to the respective Supervisor. Also know that some Investors only review short sales for approval as seldom as once per month. If Mortgage Insurance exists on the loan or it has been sold and re-sold, 90 – 120 days for an approval is typical.

I have an ENTIRE SECTION devoted to speeding things up below entitled – "Helping the Servicer Get Their Head out Of Their _____ And Make a Decision"

2) **PROBLEM - "My approval letter only gives me 2 weeks to close?"**

REASON – Loan may be going to charge off, there could be a tax payment due, or the Investor may have a payment due to the Servicer Sit tight, getting extensions on acceptance letters is not difficult.

3) **PROBLEM – "Approval letter expires and you need an extension"**

How To Solve:

Seems simple, but, JUST ASK!!! First ask your negotiator. If he/she will not help, ESCALATE ESCALATE ESCALATE!!!! Contact the executive office or the name on the approval letter.

If you are still stuck, CONTACT US!

HAVING DONE THIS FOR MANY YEARS, WE KNOW PEOPLE THAT CAN HELP!

Try these lines:

"Buyer is having an appraisal issue"

Or

"Buyer is having financing issues"

Or

"Seller needs more time to move out"

Or

"Seller needs some time to clean or repair the property"

NOTE – "Per Diem" Charges – Some acceptance letters TRY to use "Per Diem", or daily charges, to penalize you for missing a closing date. Generally speaking you can COMPLETELY ignore the "per diem" charges…these are empty threats we have yet been forced to pay.

4) PROBLEM – "I need contact information for my Negotiator or Supervisor"

How to Solve:

See "Once You Have a Negotiator" Section (or call US, we have an EXTENSIVE list of upper level contacts)

5) PROBLEM – "Servicer says I can only get 5% commission"

How to Solve:

This may or may not be true. Remember, negotiators are often just reading from their script. Try these lines:

1 - "Let me check with my broker to see if we can agree to that. I know he/she usually will not agree since we have 6% written in the SIGNED sales contract and listing agreement" – this puts you in the "same boat" as your negotiator, middle-person checking with a "boss"

Or

2 – "If I can get the Buyer to increase his/her sales price by 1%, so that the investor on this receives the same NET, can we get the 6% agreed to in the SIGNED sales contract and listing agreement?"
- noting 6% has already been agreed to IN WRITING will work with newer negotiators

Or

3 – "I spoke to my broker and he said we can NOT agree to reduce the commission on this. If this buyer walks, will you at least keep the file open so we can find a new buyer, one who will cover your shortage?"
- Many negotiators get nervous when they may have to start the file over again

Or

4 – "I asked my broker, and he/she said we closed a short sale with you guys last month and were able to get 6%. He/she asked me to see if you or the investor can make an exception.....just this once"
-back to the "just this once" exception.....this works best, particularly if you reach out to the Investor.

$ CASH TIP$ This works EXTREMELY well:

Find a local real estate attorney and partner with him or her, again, are YOU really qualified to offer legal and financial advice?

On your settlement statement, ALWAYS put in at least $1500 in attorney fees, to be split with you and the attorney. We suggest you start with at least $3500 in attorney fees so you have room for negotiating should it be necessary. Again, this will put more cash in your pocket, and, give both you and your client legal counsel throughout the process (many homeowners LOVE that they now have an attorney to work with and a letter to the Servicer from an attorney can get things done)

Of course, I would suggest whomever you work with read this course, and again, make CERTAIN they are familiar with short sales. You do NOT want your client contacting them and not knowing some basic short sale information.

Overcoming Seller Objections

With your Seller, the following objections should be addressed PRIOR to taking the listing.

Seller Objection #1 – "I will not sign a promissory note"

If you're Seller has no hardship, and will NOT agree to a promissory note, consider passing on the listing. Most banks now are REQUESTING, remember, they are only REQUESTING, that a promissory note be signed, particularly in cases where the owner refinanced and took cash out.

As noted above, ALWAYS find out from your Seller if he/she is willing to sign a promissory note and if so, up to what amount and on what terms would he/she be comfortable, i.e., $100/month, 0% interest, no pre-payment penalty. You will likely need to negotiate this once the acceptance letter is issued.

1) If the hardship is a loss of income, evidenced by the hardship letter or the financials, you should be able to get a promissory note removed altogether (remember, ESCALATE).

Try These Lines (remember, make is as easy as possible for your Negotiator to get a "Yes"):

"My Seller needs money for moving expenses"

Or

"My Seller now has bad credit and needs a large security deposit for his new home"

Or

"As you can clearly see from the financial forms submitted, my Seller is already behind on other bills, forcing him to pay a promissory note or cash will only cause further hardship"

BEST MOVE - Have the Seller put the above in writing, sign it and send it in.

At a MINIMUM, most banks will amend the terms (amount, interest rate, etc.) of the promissory note.

2) If the financials are strong -- see how much cashola the bank needs to eliminate the promissory note and release the lien (again this is negotiable just like the amount and terms of the promissory note). We can help you make a game plan thereafter once this amount is known and this option is available.

If the bank and/or mortgage insurer tell you that a promissory note MUST be signed, try:

"Mr. and Mrs. Homeowner discussed this with their attorney and were advised to let the home go to foreclosure and wait to get paid to move out…..via "Cash For Keys" "

Or

"Can we keep the file open for 3 or 4 months so the Seller can save some money to pay you?"

Or

"If that is the Investor's requirement, we will just withdraw the listing and cancel the contract…..let me check with my broker on how to do this…….what do you need from me _____(your negotiator) in order to just close this short sale?"

Seller Objection #2 - "I will not bring any cash to closing"
If they do not have cash, or, refuse to bring any cash, consider passing on the Listing unless you are prepared to give up part of your commission, or, prepared to ask the Buyer to contribute additional monies.

Seller Objection #3 – "But I am missing documents"
If a Seller has no pay stubs, or, has not filed tax returns, or is missing ANY document required for the short sale packet, have him/her simply write and sign a letter stating same (the negotiator simply needs something for the file)

Seller Objection #4 – "But I do not need to sell short"
What you WANT to say – "Really, you know more about the market than I do and we can sell your house for MORE than anyone else in the area?!?"

What you BETTER say instead (after showing them comparable, and assuming payments are not late and no foreclosure date is at hand):

"Great, let me try to sell the home for what you think it is worth. If we cannot sell it for what you think it is worth, are you open to completing a short sale?"

Your call here whether to take the listing.

Seller Objection #5 – "But it Will Ruin My Credit"
Like pain, bad credit is often temporary. Let the Seller know credit can be repaired. Ask them how important it is to get their life back in order, doing the right thing for their family financially long term. I use "Mr. Seller, what is more important, your credit or your personal wellbeing?"

Seller Objection #6 – "But What about Paying Taxes"
Tax consequences will vary, best to refer them to an accountant and mention IRS Form 982 (see link to same in the "Helpful Web Sites) section below

Seller Objection #7 – "But My House Needs Work"
No worries here, the property is sold "as-is" on a short sale, no need to fix anything.

Seller Objection #8 – "But My House IS Worth More Than I Owe"
If they are convinced they CAN get more than they owe, and you know otherwise, RUN FOR THE HILLS, or, if they ARE open to a short sale AFTER trying for a brief time at the higher price, consider moving forward.

Overcoming Servicer Objections

The key for you here is making it as easy as possible for your negotiator to get a "yes" from his/her boss (true of ANY negotiation, make it as easy as possible to say "yes" to your proposal). Also keep in mind, with time, the investor on the note will get more motivated and more cooperative. There is a reason they LOVE to hear your Buyer can close quickly.

Tell your Servicer – "No deal…..I will advise the homeowner to just let the home go to foreclosure, then, have your Investor pay them to move out via "cash for keys" Servicers HATE that line, but it ALWAYS works!!!!!!!!

Servicer Objection #1 – "Your offer is to low"

Keep in mind this is the number one (numerous Uno for my Spanish agents) objection to give you guys in the negotiator handbook or, when they are reading to you from their phone script.

Try These Lines:

"No it isn't. You're an idiot and so is the BPO agent", you will be tempted to say this at times…..don't!!! If you do, let me know I would LOVE to hear about it

Or

"Where do we need to be to get this done?"

Or

"How close are we?"

Or

"If I can get you $XXXX (increase the offer amount by 2% or 3%), how soon can you send us an acceptance letter?"

If you want to impress (and spook) your negotiator, respond with:

"Is the offer too low based on the BPO, total loss, or offer to value……?"

This will help you determine, as noted previously, if you have any acceptance, Tier I, Tier II, or Tier III approval.

Servicer Objection #2 – "Our BPO/Appraisal Came In At $XXXX (an amount too high to approve your offer)"

Your odds of this happening will be reduced if you follow what we mention above and actually MEET the BPO agent at the property as instructed above. You also should have already sent in your own BPO letter to combat and negotiate against a high BPO valuation.

However, try these lines:

"Was an interior BPO done?" – did someone go inside the property to see the condition

Or

"How long is that BPO good for?" – Most expire after 60 days and a new BPO is ordered.

Or

"Who do I need to speak with to have a new, accurate BPO done, one more reflective of the current value and 30 days to sell valuation?" – getting new BPO's is difficult, but possible

Or

"I will ask the Buyer to increase their offer to meet your required net" – this is easiest, but naturally met with resistance from the Buyer

If the valuation truly is WAY out of line, and this WILL happen, IMMEDIATELY take the issue to the big boys and make something happen in the Executive offices (we have had as many as 4 BPO's completed when necessary).

We also suggest you send a list of the showings noting how many persons visited the property and when, and, send this to the bank. When shown to the right person, most often after you have escalated your file, it always helps make your case.

There is a National Association of BPO Professionals, NABPOP, but to date, we have had NO LUCK using that as a counter negotiations point.

Servicer Objection #3 – "The Seller MUST skip or miss payments"

Tell them to send you something in writing that states:

"Owner MUST skip payments"

Legally I do not believe they can REQUIRE Sellers to miss payments, forcing them to ruin their credit. We have NEVER had a lender require this when we push back. Your negotiator only asks this b/c it makes his/her job easier and it is part of the phone script they read from.

Next time, try our standard response to the "skip payments" requirement....I LOVE THIS:

"Really, that is AWESOME!!!! I can actually tell the Seller to quit paying you guys and live in the home FOR FREE during the short sale process....they are going to be so thankful and excited about living in their home for free while we work on this short sale....."

Servicer response 9999 times out of 10000:
"Uhhhhh, I am not saying you have to skip payments......"

Bottom Line - If asked to skip payments, tell them to put something in writing for you to show the homeowner's "legal advisor" and watch them squirm....
THE TRICK - Get the Negotiator off his script and YOU OWN THEM!!!!

Servicer Objection #4 – "The Seller MUST contribute cash"

If the Seller HAS some cash to contribute (and you already know this because you pre-screened them), have him/her pay up and get to closing.

If the Seller has NO cash to contribute:
See Above - "Seller Objection #1 – I Will Not Sign a Promissory Note"
Also try some of these lines:

"We have closing set for __XX__ (where XX is 10-14 days from today), are we really going to have to re-schedule closing"

Or

"Can the Buyer contribute the cash?"

Or

"Since there is no cash to contribute, how long do I have to find a new Buyer before you guys decide to foreclose?"

Servicer Objection #5 – "We are missing documents from your short sale packet"

This may or may not be true. One of my FAVORITE lines here:

"Really, so you received page 1-7 and page 10-20, what do you think happened to page _____?"

If you put the loan number on top of every page, and, call in TWICE for fax numbers to send short sale packet to, you will GREATLY reduce the number of times you hear this Objection.

Servicer Objection #6 – We Only Pay 5% Commission to Agents

See "Overcoming Agent Issues" above. Most of the time you can get 6% OR MORE if you simply ask and push back….again, keeping in mind you want to ALWAYS make it as easy as possible for your negotiator to work WITH you on getting that 6% (we have had as much as 8% paid to agents, again, do not be afraid to ask)!!!!
Keep in mind, it RARELY makes sense for the Investor to foreclose over 1%!!!

Politely Helping the Servicer Get Their Head Out Of Their ____, And Make a Decision

This is the number one complaint for ANYONE doing short sales. Below are some of the tricks we use to help them move more quickly.

When addressing your negotiator, ALWAYS ALWAYS ALWAYS play "nice" and preface any communication, whether by phone or e-mail, with this line:
"I know you are stuck in the middle like me, but......"

"The homeowner was in tears this afternoon because of what _____ (servicer name) is putting them through......."

Or

"I got a NASTY voice mail message from the Buyer's agent this morning......."

Or

"My boss/broker just yelled at me because this is taking so long...."

Or

"The first/second lien holder is closing out the file in 7 days if they do not hear something"

Or

"We have closing set for _____, we will have to re-schedule if we do not receive an approval letter in the next 7 days"

Or

"The Buyer contacted me and is withdrawing his offer if we do not hear by _____ (even better if you get this in writing)"

Or

"The Buyer has an interest rate lock set to expire"
Or

"The Seller is meeting with a bankruptcy attorney next week. You know what happens when Sellers meet with bankruptcy attorneys."

Or

"The delays are making me look incompetent. _____ just closed a short sale with you guys and it only took _____ days......my boss/broker is mad."

Or you can use my personal favorite:

"Dear _____ (negotiator name), how about I send you and your supervisor a giant tub of Vaseline so you can GET YOUR HEAD OUT OF YOUR _____ and send me an acceptance letter so we can go to closing!!!"

Ok.......I have NEVER used that one, but, REALLY wanted to on MANY MANY occasions..........if you elect to use it, please let me know how it works!!!!

Some Great Tips For Short Sale Success:

1) When you leave a voice mail message for your negotiator (I know, they "usually" answer the phone, but play along with me here), upon completing your message:

ALWAYS HIT "#"

To send your message with urgency. Doing this will often page your negotiator, send a text message directly to their computer, and, for some it will actually send them an e-mail.....good stuff.....

2) If asked about occupancy, the best answer is -- "I believe the home is occupied" Anything else and the Servicer has the right to change the locks to protect their investment. For obvious reasons, this can be a real pain in the backside for you.

3) NEVER give out your client's phone number, tell them you do not believe you are authorized to give this out or that you need to ask your broker.
If your negotiator INSISTS on a phone number, change the last 2 numbers of the Seller's phone number:

Example:
Seller Phone Number - 703-123-4567
Becomes 703-123-4576 (again, just switching the last two numbers)

Servicers only want these numbers so they can call and harass your client for payments. Refer them back to the "Do Not Call" letter you sent in.

4) Keep Your Negotiator On Your Side:
Always close ANY correspondence to the negotiator, e-mail, voice mail, or fax cover, with:
"Thanks for all your time, efforts, and hard work on this file"

5) Great Tip – How To Establish Price:

Ask Your Negotiator – "Can you give me a "Listing Price Recommendation"?

If they say "NO", (and most will), hang up.
Call back and tell the next person that answers the phone:

"My client wants to do a deed in lieu of foreclosure. I understand the home must be listed for at least 90 days to do this, at what price shall I list the property for sale?"

How can YOU just keep asking and asking and asking and asking WITHOUT being a 4 year old?!?!

We call it – "Being Professionally Persistent"!!!

Call your negotiator every day (even 2-3 times a day):

Call in, leave a message, then call back and say:

"I think you forget to leave the _____ (account number, your call back number, your fax number) on my last message, so I am calling you back……"
Or try:
"I just missed a call from this number, was not sure if it was you calling me back with an approval…...."

(You can also do this with emails by "forgetting" to leave the account number, the address, the Seller's name, etc.)!!

7 More "Weapons" To Use In Getting Your Short Sale Approved:

1) **Great line to negotiator when things are dragging out:**

"If you were me, what would you do next?"

2) **Great line to negotiator for approval extensions:**

"I need an extension on the acceptance letter. The seller needs time to move, clean, or repair the property"

3) **Great line to negotiator when things are dragging out:**

"Did someone from my office upset someone because it has been weeks since we heard anything?"

4) **Great line to negotiator when you are close on the numbers:**

"_____(negotiator name), great news, i got your investor another $1000, $2000 because the buyer agreed to increase his offer, the agents are kicking in money, the seller is taking money from his retirement, borrowing from a friend, etc."

5) **Great move if you are no longer authorized, but were just days ago:**

Call back to the exact same number and try again. Negotiators are all over the country and most of the time you suddenly will be authorized. Again, many negotiators spend their time surfing the internet and the quickest way to get rid of you, tell you they are not authorized to speak with you….this happens most frequently if you call in late in the day.

6) **Great tip if you send documents via e-mail to your negotiator:**

Be certain to also fax them in to the general "800" number so they are put into the main imaging system. Documents sent directly to your negotiator via e-mail may or may not be imaged, meaning if your negotiator should quit, items you sent to him or her could be lost and gone forever…..ask me how i learned this?

7) Great Tip:

If you lose a home to foreclosure, that did have a short sale offer in, have them put it in writing. It will give your Seller legal re-course should the Servicer decide to come after the Seller for deficiency liens in the future (they can tell the judge you WERE willing to pay things off and make things right, but, the Servicer would not permit them to do so, this may even work with a foreclosure being reported on one's credit)

My Favorite E-Mail Ever

Yes these have actually been sent in, and, on 3 occasions now, we were "banished" from ever doing business with these Servicers

When I say "banished", I mean it!!! Twice I have received e-mails from Executive Offices, stating:

"Please note, we will no longer be dealing with you or your company"

REEEEEAAALLLLLLYYYY, no chance I will stop helping homeowners get through these tough times and YES we still do business with both Servicers currently!!!

When we go to bat for clients, they get 100% commitment to getting them through this challenging time in their lives….no exceptions……I hope you share this commitment.

The messages below are intended to be used ONLY when all other avenues have failed, and, try as you must, the Servicer just cannot seem to get the Investor to make the right decision.

My Personal Favorite E-Mail Message: "Is The Investor On This Smarter Than A Fifth Grader…?"

The message below went out to almost 40 persons at Wells Fargo after we were getting jerked around. We heard from 2 of the higher ups within 24 hours and had an approval letter less than 7 days later.

Sent to:

ALL your Servicer contacts including the Investor if you were able to learn who this is, and, to the OCC, Office of the Comptroller of the Currency (they regulate banks).

And a "cc" to:

The Seller, any agents involved in the transaction, the Title Company, attorney, etc

Subject Line of the E-mail:

"Is The Investor on This Smarter than a Fifth Grader….I Think Not?"

Actual Message Sent:

> Regarding:
>
> Jeffrey _____
> Washington DC 20020
>
>
> To all interested parties,
>
> So I do not waste any more of my time, the seller's time, the seller's agent's time, the buyer and buyer agent's time, or that of the attorney and title company, here is where we stand:
>
> ASC/Wells Fargo the first lien holder will NOT allow more than 10% in TOTAL closing costs inclusive of:
>
>> Payoff to the second lien holder (OCWEN)
>> Agent fees
>> Washington DC City and county deed stamps
>> Washington DC delinquent real estate taxes
>> General closing costs
>> Fees to me for all HELPING THEM MITIGATE THEIR LOSSES!!!!

To review the HUD (see attached), the offer price we have is $270,000 (for the record it is HIGHER than the BPO number) and reflects:

6% -- OCWEN (second lien holder) - is owed $115,000, has agreed to $15000

5% -- Agents -- $13,500 - already taking a discount from the normal 6%, I have NO IDEA why agents even bother with short sales when there are TONS of other properties available for sale that pay full commission and do not take 5 months to complete

1% - Washington DC City and county deed stamps, $3729, NO WAY around this

1% - -Delinquent real estate taxes, $1628, NO WAY around this and will continue to increase

The above leaves NOTHING for any general closing costs and NOTHING for my company's time and efforts having worked on this case since May, and my efforts again to HELP OCWEN AND ASC/WELLS FARGO.

The 10% policy is just dumb and will cost investors MILLIONS of dollars if this is how things continue to work

It has been admitted by 4 persons now at Wells that the 10% is not only foolish, but, that by taking back the property they will lose FAR MORE MONEY, YET EVERYONE SEEMS TO WANT TO PUT THEIR HEAD IN THE SAND AND SAY:

"Oh Well, Not Our Problem"

To all parties involved herewith, I quite honestly am tired of the games and non-sense we have been put through thus far and if it were not for my client, Mr. Kuhn, I would tell ASC and Wells to close this case, take back the property, and go ahead lose more than they will by doing the right thing and accepting the offer.

 Back to my original question (See Subject Line):

My answer is a resounding "NO", the investor here is clearly NOT SMARTER THAN A FIFTH GRADER!!

Why -- Even a Fifth Grader can see that losing less money now is FAR BETTER than losing more money later!!!

The fact that the ASC/Wells Fargo BPO came in LOWER THAN THE CURRENT OFFER CLEARLY EXEMPLIIFIES THIS FACT!!

I rest my case......To all parties, please advise me how best to proceed or if we should simply move our efforts elsewhere....letting the property go to foreclosure.

Sincerely,
Ben Benita

Other Great E-Mails

Sent to:

The Seller, any agents involved in the transaction, the Title Company, attorney, etc

And a "cc" to:

ALL your Servicer contacts including the Investor if you were able to learn who this is, and, to the OCC, Office of the Comptroller of the Currency (they regulate banks).

Subject Line of the E-mail:

"Sorry _____ (Servicer) does not care about your _____ (Seller's hardship)"

Or

"As we discussed _____ (Servicer) just keeps robbing the investor for servicing fees" – send the Investor a "cc" with this subject line and watch what happens

Or

"I know the BPO agent just wants the listing and is not NABPOP certified"

Or

"I am not certain why _____ (Servicer) is ignoring us"

Or, with missed payments:

"I know this has taken _____ (months), but at least you can keep living in the home for free"

Message to Send:

"Dear _____ (Seller),

I continue to do my best with _____ (Servicer), but, despite my best efforts we continue to be ignored.

As we discussed, and, since you will soon be facing foreclosure, I would STRONGLY urge you to file a formal complaint with the following regulatory agencies, including:

> Consumer Finance Protection Bureau - CFPB
> State Attorney General -

And also file a complaint with the Office of the Comptroller of the Currency (they regulate the loan Servicers):

> http://www.OCC.treas.gov/
> to e-mail OCC -- Publicaffairs3@occ.treas.gov,

To file a complaint through the OCC, use their complaint web site:

> www.helpwithmybank.gov, start here, online customer complaint form, helpwithmybank.faq@occ.treas.gov

You can also go to these web sites to see some of the horror stories others have had with _____ (Servicer):

> www.Complaints.com
> www.Ripoffreport.com
> www.BorrowerHelp.com

Sincerely,

You

PS. At least if they foreclose this will have NOT been a TOTAL WASTE OF TIME. Again, as I advised you, _____ (Servicer) will actually offer you some money via "cash for keys" to move out of the home!!!

**Bonus - Four Other Effective E-Mail Subject Lines

With e-mails SENT to all of your Servicer contacts and a "cc" to the owner and real estate agents:

If the owner has missed payments:

E-mail Subject Line - "_____missed payments and counting, _____ (Seller) DOES appreciate being able to live in the home for free, but, would like to get this done and move on"

Or

<u>**E-mail Subject Line**</u> - "Can anyone tell us why we are being ignored?"

Or

E-mail Subject Line - "As we discussed, it looks like it is time to file a formal complaint with the Office of the Comptroller of the Currency and the _____ (your state) Attorney General"

Or

E-mail Subject Line - "_____ (Seller) does appreciate getting to live in the home for _____ (number of payments missed) months for free, but would now like to get this to closing and move on"

Helpful Web Sites:

To see if a loan is held by:

>   Fannie Mae - http://loanlookup.fanniemae.com/loanlookup/
>   Freddie Mac - https://ww3.freddiemac.com/corporate/

When there is a Private Investor on the Loan, Best to Visit:

>   https://www.mers-servicerid.org/sis/

To File Formal Complaints against ANY Servicer:

>   http://www.consumerfinance.gov/

To Find Servicer Contacts For Free

Assuming you are NOT working with us for some reason:

>   Google _____ (your Servicer) contacts
>   Google _____ (your Servicer) stock symbol
>   www.Yellowpages.com

If You Want To Pay For Servicer Contacts:

>   www.jigsaw.com
>   www.LinkedIn.com (get their PREMIUM Service)

If you're Seller has a VA loan:

For information on the Service-members Civil Relief Act (SCRA):

>   http://usmilitary.about.com/od/sscra/l/blscramenu.htm

For information on the VA Compromise Loan (For Seller's with VA Loans):

>   http://www.valoans.com/va_article.cfm?id=140

If You Want To Find Complaints about Your Servicer (good ammunition when negotiating):

On occasion it helps to send via e-mail or fax, some complaints the Servicer has received already (most could care less, but, it can help)

Google "_____ (Servicer Name) Complaints"

> www.Complaints.com
> www.Ripoffreport.com
> www.BorrowerHelp.com - to look up complaint issues against a lender

For Filing Complaints against Your Servicer:

> Consumer Finance Protection Bureau – CFPB, 855-411-2372
> http://www.consumerfinance.gov/

For Filing Complaints against Your Servicer:

> The Office of the Comptroller of the Currency (OCC):
>
> www.OCC.Treas.gov/
> E-mail the OCC – PublicAffairs3@OCC.Treas.Gov
> Contact - 800-613-6743
>
> To file a complaint through the OCC:
>
> www.Helpwithmybank.gov
> E-mail them - Helpwithmybank.faq@occ.treas.gov
>
> Office of Thrift Supervision (OTS)
>
> www.OTS.Treas.Gov
> E-mail – Consumer.complaint@OTS.Treas.Gov
> http://www.ots.treas.gov/
> Contact – 800-842-6929

For Information about Tax Consequences:

> Contact a local CPA (another GREAT referral source) and check out:
> http://www.irs.gov/pub/irs-pdf/f982.pdf

In Closing

I hope you have enjoyed this updated guide and that you are able to help more Homeowners!!!

There are thousands of families out there still struggling financially, going through challenging times and looking to you for help!!!

I hope this guide allows you to help each and every one of them avoid foreclosure, and, get their lives back on track.

Sample Documents

What follows are sample documents for you to use as you wish, including:

1) **Pre-Listing Questionnaire**

   - Should you even take the listing?

2) **Short Sale Information Page, Seller**

   - For you to send in WITH your short sale packet

3) **Short Sale Information Page, Agent**

   - For YOUR records, assuming you are NOT working with us and have online tracking abilities

4) **Estimated Short Sale and Attorney Processing Fees**

   - For working with a local attorney and justifying payment

5) **Do Not Call Letter**

   - If your client has missed payments and is getting collection calls, this letter works for ANY type of harassing creditor phone calls

6) **Qualified Written Request**

   - To find out who the Investor and mortgage Insurer is on the note, and, contact information therefor.

7) **Letter To HOA/Condo Board For Delinquent Fees**

   - Used to "short sell" delinquent HOA and/or condo association fees

8) BPO/VALUATION Challenge Letter

- Used to request a new property valuation

9) <u>Buyer Pre-Offer Questionnaire</u>

- Used when deciding whether or not to make an offer.

Pre-Listing Questionnaire

<u>Things to know BEFORE agreeing to a short sale listing:</u>

1) Why are you doing a short sale, would you prefer to stay in the property?
(If "yes", consider a loan modification, do what is best for the Client)

ANSWER -

_____

_____

_____

2) are you behind on payments and is there a foreclosure date forthcoming?

ANSWER -

_____

_____

_____

3) How many liens are on your home?

ANSWER -

_____

_____

_____

4) Who are the liens with (mortgage, taxes, HOA)?

ANSWER -

_____

_____

_____

6) Are the taxes current?

ANSWER -

_____

_____

_____

7) Do you have any pending litigation?

ANSWER -

_____

_____

_____

8) Have you spoken with a bankruptcy attorney?

ANSWER -

_____

_____

_____

9) Are you willing to bring cash to closing in order to avoid foreclosure?

ANSWER -

_____

_____

_____

10) Are you willing to sign a promissory note in order to avoid foreclosure?

ANSWER -

_____

_____

_____

11) Will you agree to the possible tax consequences in order to avoid foreclosure?

ANSWER -

_____

_____

_____

12) What are your plans when the short sale is complete (where will you live)?

ANSWER -

_____

_____

_____

13) Do you know anyone else that I might be able to help with their property? (You should be asking this no matter what)

ANSWER -

_____

_____

_____

If the answers above are NOT favorable, consider passing on the listing.

NOTE - Is or was your client in the military? If "yes", find out if he/she is eligible for a VA Compromise Sale (ask the Servicer about the Service members Civil Relief Act (SCRA) – (replaces the Soldiers and Sailors Civil Relief Act of 1940)
VA Compromise Sale – a short sale for Veterans whereby the VA pays the difference between what is owed and what the home sells for.

Short Sale Information Page, Seller

(Send In With Your Short Sale Packet behind Your Cover Page)

Seller - _____

Address - _____

Property Status - _____

Reason for Sale/Hardship -_____

Date Submitted-_____

FIRST LIEN

Lender Name - _____

Loan Number - _____

Loan Type - _____

Amount Owed - _____

Amount Offered - _____

SECOND LIEN

Lender Name - _____

Loan Number - _____

Loan Type - _____

Amount Owed - _____

Amount Offered - _____

Listing Agent (for Interior BPO access) – Name, Number, E-mail

BPO Contact (if different from above) - Name, Number, E-mail

Where to Send Acceptance – Name, Phone Number, Fax, E-mail

Current Buyer(s) - _____

Short Sale Information Page, Agent
(For Your Records)

Name of Home Owner 1: _____

Social Security Number # _____

Phone Numbers For:

Home _____ Work _____ Cell _____

Fax _____ Email _____

Name of Home Owner 2: _____

Social Security Number # _____

Phone Numbers For:

Home _____ Work _____ Cell _____

Fax _____ Email _____

Short Sale Property Address:

_____

_____

Foreclosure Auction Date (if scheduled) _____

Hardship/Reason for short sale - _____

How long have they owned the property? _____

Are they still living there? _____

First Mortgage Company _____

Amount owed on first mortgage $_____

How many payments behind? _____

Loan type - -FHA, VA, Conventional, Uninsured

Account Number _____

Investor on the Note: _____

Mortgage Insurance – Yes_____ No _____

Mortgage Insurance Company - _____

Mortgage Insurance Coverage Ratio - _____

Date Short Sale Submitted - _____

Second Mortgage Company _____

Amount owed on first mortgage $_____

How many payments behind? _____

Loan type - -FHA, VA, Conventional, Uninsured

Account Number _____

Investor on the Note: _____

Mortgage Insurance – Yes_____ No _____

Mortgage Insurance Company - _____

Mortgage Insurance Coverage Ratio - _____

Date Short Sale Submitted - _____

Are there other Liens on the property (list)?

Amount Owed: $ _____

To: _____

Property Taxes Due:

Amount Owed: $ _____

To: _____

Is there a Home Owner's Association? _____

     Are the payments current? _____

     If not, how much is due? _____

List of repairs needed on the property:

_____

_____

_____

_____

_____

_____

_____

_____

_____

Approximate cost of needed repairs: $_____

Is there a redemption period in the state where the property is located? _____

If "yes", how long? _____

Sales Contract Offer Amount: $_____

Net First Lien: $_____

Net Second Lien: $_____

Attorney Contact Information –

Name: _____

Phone Numbers For:

Work _____ Cell _____

Fax _____ email _____

Estimated Short Sale and Attorney Processing Fees
(Second page of short sale package)

$_____.

Seller: _____

Property Address: _____

Loan Number: _____

Short Sale Processing is inclusive of:

1) Informing Seller how the short sale process works, what to expect, and any potential consequences thereof
2) Informing Seller's agent how the short sale process works.
3) Coordinating general short sale efforts with Seller and Seller's agent
4) Document collection
5) Short Sale package assembly
6) Short sale package fax coordination
7) Necessary follow up phone calls to _____] Lender(s)]
8) Short sale case escalation as needed
9) General short sale consulting as needed throughout the process to all parties, including Seller, Seller's agent, Buyer, Buyer's agent, title company et. All.
10) Contact as needed with foreclosure attorneys

*Hours to complete based on short sale timeline given by Lender of 90 to 120 days

Sample Do Not Call Letter

DATE

You're Address
You're Loan Number

To whom it may concern,

My attorney advised me to contact you in writing.

In accordance with the Fair Debt Collection Practices Act 805(c), please allow this to serve as formal notice to stop calling me at _____ (your phone number).

I do not wish to proceed with formal legal action against _____ (Name of creditor(s), but, will not hesitate to do so, as you will now be in direct violation of FTC Regulations.

Sincerely,

QWR Sample Letter

Certified First Class U.S. Mail Ref. # 1234 5678

<u>Correspondence Address:</u>
Institution
Address
Address

In the Matter of:
John and Jane Doe

Property Address:
123 Any Street
Atlanta, GA 30030

Account Number # <u>0000000000000</u>

R.E.S.P.A. QUALIFIED WRITTEN REQUEST

Dear Sir or Madam:

Please treat this letter as a "qualified written request" under the Federal Servicer Act, which is a part of the Real Estate Settlement Procedures Act, 12 U.S.C. 2605(e).

Specifically, we are disputing a) the identity of a true secured lender/creditor, <u>and</u> b) the existence of debt, <u>and</u> c) your authority and capacity to collect on behalf of the alleged lender/creditor. Because of extensive criminal activity and fraud in this arena, we require proof of the chain of secured ownership from the original alleged lender/creditor to the alleged current lender/creditor. Further, we require proof that you are the entity that has been contracted to work on behalf of the alleged lender/creditor.

Pursuant to "Subtitle E Mortgage Servicing" of the Dodd-Frank Wall Street Reform and Consumer Protection Act and pursuant to 12 U.S.C. Section 2605(e) (1) (A) and Reg. X Section 3500.21(e) (1), please provide:

1. A full, double sided, certified "true and accurate" copy of the original promissory note and security instrument and <u>all</u> assignments of the security instrument.

2. Full name, address and telephone number of the actual entity that funded the transaction.

3. Full name of Trust where the Note Number is trading, or has traded, and the identifying Series of Certificates.
(Note: If the note number is being traded in a Fannie Mae Trust or Freddie Mac Trust, please provide all information to identify the Trust (i.e. Fannie Mae Pool Number, CUSIP Number, REMIC or SMBS Trust Number and Trust Class/Tranche).

4. Full name, address, and telephone number of the Trustee.

5. Full name, address, and telephone number of the **Custodian of my original Promissory Note**, including the name, address and telephone number of any trustee or other fiduciary. This request is being made pursuant to Section 1641(f) (2) of the Truth in Lending Act.

6. Full name, address, and telephone number of the **Custodian of my original Security Instrument**, including the name, address and telephone number of any trustee or other fiduciary. This request is being made pursuant to Section 1641(f) (2) of the Truth in Lending Act.

7. A **physical location (address) of the original promissory note, original security instrument, and all assignments** of the security instrument, and a **contact name and phone number of someone who can arrange for inspection** of said documents.

8. Full name, address and telephone number of any master servicers, servicers, sub-servicers, contingency servicers, back-up servicers or special servicers for this account.

9. The electronic MERS number assigned to this account if this is a MERS Designated Account.

10. **Proof of true sale of the note** from alleged Lender to investors, by showing:
Wire transfer document(s), and/or
Signed purchase and sale agreement(s),
Bank statements or similar documentation.

11. The MERS Milestone Report, if the note number and security instrument was tracked by Mortgage Electronic Registration Systems. I want to see the audit trail of the alleged transfer in ownership and alleged transfer in security interest.

12. A complete audit history from alleged loan origination, showing the dates payments were applied, and to what internal accounts (i.e. principal, interest, suspense, escrow, etc.) payments were applied.

13. A complete and itemized statement of all advances or charges against this account.

14. A complete and itemized statement of the escrow for this account, if any, from the date of the note origination to the date of your response to this letter.

15. Have you purchased and charged to the account any Force-Placed Insurance?

16. A complete and itemized statement from the date of the note origination to the date of your response to this letter of the amounts charged for any forced-placed insurance, the date of the charge, the name of the insurance company, the relation of the insurance company to you or a related company, the amount of commission you received for each force-placed insurance event, and an itemized statement of any other expenses related thereto.

17. A complete and itemized statement from the date of the note origination to the date of your response to this letter of any suspense account entries and/or any corporate advance entries related in any way to this account.

18. A complete and itemized statement from the date of the loan to the date of your response to this letter of any property inspection fees, property preservation fees, broker opinion fees, appraisal fees, bankruptcy monitoring fees, or other similar fees or expenses related in any way to this loan.

19. A statement/provision under the security instrument and/or note that authorizes charging any such fee against the account.

20. Copies of all property inspection reports and appraisals, broker price opinions, and associated bills, invoices, and checks or wire transfers in payment thereof.

21. Complete copy of any transaction report(s) indicating any charges for any "add on products" sold to the debtors in connection with this account from the date of the note origination to the date of your response to this letter.

22. Complete and itemized statement of any late charges added to this account from the date of the note origination to the date of your response to this letter.

23. Complete and itemized statement of any fees incurred to modify, extend, or amend the loan or to defer any payment or payments due under the terms of the loan, from the date of the note origination to the date of your response to this letter.

24. Complete, itemized statement of the current amount needed to pay-off the alleged "loan" in full.

25. Verification of any notification provided to me of a change in servicer.

You should be advised that within FIVE (5) DAYS you must send us a letter stating that you received this letter. After that time you have THIRTY (30) DAYS to fully respond as per the time frame mandated by Congress, in "Subtitle 'E' Mortgage Servicing" of the "Dodd-Frank Wall Street Reform and Consumer Protection Act and pursuant to 12 U.S.C. Section 2605(e)(1)(A) and Reg. X Section 3500.21(e)(1).

TRUTH – IN-LENDING ACT § 131(f) (2)
Pursuant to 15 U.S.C. § 1641 (f):

Please provide the name, address and telephone number of the owner(s) of the mortgage and the master servicer of the mortgage.

You should be advised that Violations of this Section provide for statutory damages of up to $4,000 and reasonable legal fees. The amendments also clearly provide that the new notice rules are enforceable by private right of action. _15 USC 1641_

Sincerely,

_____   _____
John Doe   Date

_____   _____
Jane Doe   Date

cc:
U.S. Certified Mail # _____
Office of RESPA and Interstate Land Sales
Office of Housing, Room 9154
US Department of Housing and Urban Development
451 Seventh Street, SW
Washington, DC 2041

If Fannie Mae or Freddie Mac:

U.S. Certified Mail # _____
FHFA Office of Inspector General
Attn: Office of Investigation - Hotline
400 7th Street, SW
Washington, DC 20024

And

Fannie Mae: **OR**

U.S. Certified Mail # _____
Timothy Mayopoulos, CEO
Federal National Mortgage Association
3900 Wisconsin Avenue NW
Washington, DC 20016-2892

Freddie Mac:

U.S. Certified Mail # _____
Donald H. Layton, CEO
Federal Home Loan Mortgage Corp.
Attn: Consumer Care
8200 Jones Branch Drive
Mailcode: C1K
McLean, VA 22102

What Happens if the Servicer Fails to Respond?

Any time the Servicer fails to ACKNOWLEDGE and/or RESPOND or RESPOND COMPLETELY within the required time frame,

1) Send another letter **and**
2) Send a complaint **with** your QWR **and** the Answer to the QWR (*or report non-response*) to:

U.S. Certified Mail # _____
Consumer Financial Protection Bureau
P.O. Box 4503
Iowa City, Iowa 52244
There is a special unit inside CFPB.

Please report your results to Operation Rest.

<u>**Not necessary, but will notify the Monitor about violations**</u>:

U.S. Certified Mail # _____
Joseph A. Smith, Jr.,
Monitor of the National Mortgage Settlement
Office of Mortgage Settlement Oversight
301 Fayetteville St., Suite 1801
Raleigh, NC 27601

Each failure of the servicer to properly respond creates a cause of action for you against the servicer. That could be $2,000 statutory per violation plus actual damages plus attorney fees for each separate request. If you live in a judicial foreclosure state, the failed responses become counterclaims as part of the answer filed by your attorney. If you live in a non-judicial state, then Section 6 of RESPA allows a homeowner to file an affirmative action within one year for a mishandled Qualified Written Request.

Recommendation:

If the Servicer fails to respond to the first Qualified Written Request, send another QWR, stating that the prior request(s) dated X and Y were ignored (remember each failure creates a circumstance in which the homeowner can receive damages).

Sample Letter to HOA/ Condo Board For Delinquent Fees

Attn: _____
(HOA/Condo or other Lien Holder Contact)

Date: _____

RE: _____
(Homeowner Name)

_____
(Subject Property Address)

To whom it may concern,

My company, _____, is handling the short sale negotiations for the above referenced property, and, we FINALLY received approval letters from the first and second mortgage lien holders.

It has since come to our attention that you are owed funds for unpaid dues, and, as per the lenders, we are prepared to offer $_____ (start **LOW**) as payment in full, all cash payable at closing. (Estimated to be within 30 days of hearing back from you).

Benefits To Acceptance:

> 1 – You get <u>ALL CASH</u> at closing
> 2 – Avoids you're having to track down and attempt to collect funds from _____(Homeowner), who is already having trouble keeping up with other payments.
> 3 – Allows us to get to closing as soon as possible, which also means **<u>getting you a paying homeowner sending you a check each month.</u>**

Failure to come to terms will result in further delays and, foreclosure to the property. If the home goes to foreclosure, it could be 6 to 8 months before the property fully completes the foreclosure process and someone starts paying you again:

> Home goes to foreclosure auction
> Home gets taken back by the Investor
> Home gets listed for sale in a VERY SLOW market
> New Buyer is found and closes thereon

Let's do the right thing and agree to the above.

Let's get you paid, and, get you a new paying Homeowner as quickly as possible.

Please send a letter of approval to me directly via:

E-mail – _____

Fax – _____

Feel free to contact me at the number below with any questions.

Sincerely,

Sample BPO Challenge Letter

Seller - _____

Address - _____

Loan - _____

To Whom It May Concern,

My name is _____. I am the listing agent for the above referenced property and have been a licensed Realtor for _____ years.

It has recently come to my attention that the BPO/appraisal valuation recently came in higher than the current offer amount. I have checked with the Buyer and was told they cannot go any higher. My Broker REALLY wants me to get this done so I am hoping you can help.

(OPTIONAL PARAGRAPH) - As I am certain it was noted on the interior valuation report, the property currently needs approximately $_____ in repairs to be in fair marketable condition. _____ (EXPLAIN REPAIRS)

We have had the home listed for sale now for _____ days and have received only the one offer submitted to you for approval. For the Investor's convenience, I have included several comparable properties below for your review.

Let's do the right thing here and order a new valuation, help your Investor avoid taking back another property, and, most importantly, help _____ (HOMEOWNER) get through what is proving to be the most difficult financial time of their lives.

For interior BPO/appraisal access, feel free to contact me directly at:
Phone - _____
E-mail - _____

Thank you for your time, efforts, and understanding.

Sincerely,

Buyer Pre-Offer Questionnaire

Things EVERY Buyer should know BEFORE making an offer on a short sale:

1) Who is handling the short sale negotiations?

_____

_____

_____

2) How many short sales have they closed previously (VERIFY THIS)?

_____

_____

_____

3) How many liens are on the property?

_____

_____

_____

4) Has title been pulled to verify liens?

_____

_____

_____

5)   Have   any   documents   yet   been   submitted   to   the   bank?

_____

_____

_____

6) Are payments current and if not, how many payments have been missed?

_____

_____

_____

7) Is there a foreclosure date set currently?

_____

_____

_____

8) Does the Seller have cash to contribute to the short sale?

_____

_____

_____

9) Will the Seller agree to a promissory note and possible tax consequences?

_____

_____

_____

10) Will the Seller permit Buyer or Buyer's Agent to speak with the Lender directly?

_____

_____

_____

Recommended Partners

Recommended Partners – Short Sale Tracking

Before doing ANY short sale, be certain to have tracking ability to record ANY AND ALL contact you make with the Servicer, including faxes sent to what number and when, who you called and what number(s) you called to reach people, etc. Systems and tracking will prove essential with short sales and comes in VERY handy when you ever need to "escalate" your file.

We use, and strongly recommend, using Short Sale Commander (also known as Realty Commander, www.ShortSaleCommander.com, or www.RealtyCommander.com, or call 800-658-3420 and tell them "Ben Benita sent you"!

Recommended Partners – General Information:

When You Are Looking For Short Sale Packets, or, For General Short Sale Assistance, Please Visit:

www.ShortSaleSuperstars.com

This site is run by our good friend Bryant Tutas, a laid back "beach-bum" who has altered the face of short sales all over the country.

Recommended Partners

Recommended Partners – Technical Tips:

For "Technical Tips", or to stay up on current short sales news, another great resource, on Facebook:

> Short Sale Masterminds

This site is by invite only and is run by Kevin Lancaster, one of the brightest minds in the nation on the topic of short sales.

When you join, be sure to tell him Ben Benita sent you!!!

Recommended Partners – General Information:

When You Are Looking For Short Sale Packets, or, For General Short Sale Assistance, Please Visit:

> www.Short-Sale-Specialists.com

This site is run by our friend Mike Linkenauger, a great guy and one of the best people to turn to for short sale marketing in the country.

www.ingramcontent.com/pod-product-compliance
Lightning Source LLC
Chambersburg PA
CBHW081745200326
41597CB00024B/4398